Meridians

Meridians

poems

Cameron McGill

Acme Poem Company
Willow Springs Books
Spokane, Washington

Meridians is part ten in the Acme Poem Company Surrealist Poetry Series.

Cataloging and Publication Information available from the Library of Congress on request.

Edited: Christopher Howell
Cover Artwork: Adapted from Henri-Edmond Cross's *Landscape with Stars*, courtesy of The Metropolitan Museum of Art, New York, Robert Lehman Collection, 1975
Cover Design: Caitlin Feldman
Interior Design: Caitlin Feldman

FIRST EDITION

Willow Springs Books, Spokane, WA 99202
Copyright © 2020 Cameron McGill
Printed in the United States of America
All Rights Reserved
Printed by Gray Dog Press
ISBN: 978-0-9990050-8-8

This and other Willow Springs Books publications may be viewed online at willowspringsbooks.org.

for Brian and Sam

Contents

He brought the compass from the ship
left it on the table
took off his cap
took off his shoes
couldn't sleep.
Where are the four points of the horizon
where is the body's center . . .

—Yannis Ritsos, translated by Edmund Keeley

44.6336° N, 86.2345° W

Michigan open your dark umbrella
your benzedrined nightsky

Give me the mind slipping from my hands
gravel roads beyond county lines & the rain's understanding
Where I am full as a pupil & miniature
in the moonlight   I have come home

This house in cloudshadow is language
is I empty my pockets & my life
There are twelve rivers inside my body
I drown in eleven of them   One
brings me to you

I keep a small light where the madmen can't
touch it   The dogs can't touch it

The dock's thin arm reaching to the lake drops the moon like a yolk
I let go the dark   that you would come
take me by the hand to a field
I wait now among a stand of pines
so that anywhere I go will be a clearing

INVENTIONS TOWARD PLEASURE

Cardinal points drum down slaked waves to crumble at my feet. The soul is when the body's inside looks the same as out, only behind glass. My feet underwater, mirror clear. I read once when humans die off, so too will sadness—our second invention toward pleasure. Some things insist more than we do—clutches of birds at sundown in southern panic, lastlight tearing like lions of color at the trees from dunes to pier. Beauty, our first—wildword in summer, dangerous perennial. Our bodies made both—helpless pilots amongst a shake of pine, tiers upon tiers of career-ending violets.

44.6336° N, 86.2345° W

Morning expands one rib at a time
speaks through the pinktops of pines   On the porch
I write to a friend whose mother has passed
Blue fog is a doe that startles
at my cough   I drink black water from its eye

This isn't about halfdreamt things
The veil over the lake about to boil a man
It's too quiet to answer anything but the tonguecolors
of the east   fernlight slices from a mandoline

My words are bad acreage
I think of taking my friend's grief   holding it
above my head & wading out   It is clear I can see the sand
I tell myself this is helping   this is what the heart looks like working

Each step   the outbreath
There is a boat & a man moving his line
He's throwing longer & longer threads
to the still dark

MOONFLOWER

I think of you here, where the forest swallows light,
where crosses on the highway are religion's limits.
The deer carcass calls to the crows.
Tires on wet pavement scatter them
to what lent-purple light is left in the west.
They settle in eaves like vowels from the dead.
This awful forest, home to dark engines—
to those who speak in hoarded consonants,
to *Spring* which isn't Latin for *things un-die*.
What are you growing in me, God,
where your green apron darkens?
Did I always close to the sun
even before there was one?

40.1164° N, 88.2434° W

I think of youth as one long summer
incorrectly   Mornings the gray of a horse's pink tongue
Farmers calling in the corn from Thomasboro
surrounded by harvests   tall as men gaunting doorways
of train stations   sunburnt & matchless at Logan & Water

I've grown away from you
slowly like a fingernail   Where is my sister
in her torrential blond   Running skinny in the yard
with the neighbor boy who'd later hang himself

How I didn't try to love him
who torpedoed by sadness & psychiatry chased me home
yelling all his mind at the street
The decrepit limousine our lives had been

Here is a promise the length of my body
that you will take me like a silo   of smoke leaving
the cigarette in my father's hand

The dreams I had forgive me
When spring's tornadoes came we raced
with paper to the basement
& drew them

AFTER WORK

My father would split his attention
With an icepick. Crush four fingers
Of a tumbler, light ten cigarettes
Like birthday candles, blow them out in front of me.

He'd offer me the olives—each round
Bitter, salt and ethyl on my tongue—a truce
Without words. I understood

What was agreed upon
Those nights when two
Unlikely things were forced together—
I'd slip the slick red hearts from their cavities.
I was a kid; I was helping.

44.6336° N, 86.2345° W

This is not a nightmare this is how the world looks
in a forest at night   phantasmagoric
in the canopy   There is the sound of sleet ticking on bark
Bark that quakes like tuning forks
in the crowns of pine   Crowns like the heads of waves
seen by no one

but my father & me
in the four o'clock dark   He starts in with noises
of his life   A fluency of branches swimming at the window
means I wake in blue   The room a vanity mirror with rain on it

Downstairs he rises with his cough
His small lamp hung in the dark   Who smokes must be
talking to himself   There is a freighter skulking full of ore
pounding sleepknots to Charlevoix

This distant country called me home
Why have I only brought it adjectives

I try to sleep
She is not next to me I cannot   put my hand on her back
I have only a stormful   of trees in the dark

DRUNK WITH ZODIAC

for Cyd

Taurus charges in the dark like Oregon,
horns the width of this beer with a moon.

I forget where I live, keep repeating your name.
Its gray dissolve in rain at night is fair.

Paradise Ridge fogged in breath, a bad health
and ice-lungs of pine. Orion is a butterfly

turned on its wing, pinned against boredom
and black paper. Our bodies cut askew,

shiver up and to the west, ricocheted
and charcoal-burnt as maps. The myth

of beasts unseen, animations on the night:

> Fronds of bracken hung like hair
> of the subway cellist, legs spread and hugging;

> The boxer's head thrown back,
> nose bloody gushing stars; The young

> woman breastfeeding who's fallen asleep;
> Gaunt man seated, finger raised, recalls

> certain beauty of youth; Your birthmark
> like a thin fox torn across the sky.

> And what of that shooting one: my twin
> whose streak shirks blur—the runner

> giving chase, whose feet cannot be seen.

41.9740° N, 87.6782° W

I'm less the buildings I used to live in
& more the strangers passing in their windows—
the woman dancing with her baby   holding him high
a man carrying laundry to the bedroom with a beer

I return your shadow
to where I found it in me   beside chimneys
on Damen Avenue   in an alley piling breath into January

I live in too much silence—
there needs to be someone in the car the room the bed   The world
in its heartbreak of mastery wants me undone

To come here knowing nothing
should want to speak   except the wind & frost on the grass
in shadows of trees on Winnemac   This all starts to sound the same—
the city the block
my assurances   The deficits they make of memory

Yesterday I met the woman I'd lived with for years
My remembering a bath
her knees islands in the cooling water   I'm afraid
describing things ruins them   That's not true It was me
who asked what the body wanted & didn't
listen for the answer

AN AGREEMENT

From a loose nail in the wall
I hang a picture of two silos filled with moonlight.
I imagine rain through the streetlights behind them.

Their inner reaches stretch before my birth. A blur
at the edge walking out of frame
says, *filled with joy is a possibility, wife is a question.*

I stand in the room like a man balancing
in the back of a box-truck his life.
I run my fingers along the inside of September,
remove strings from the piano, silver hairs from my temple.

In the silos' shadow, I want understanding
and the empire of memory
separate. Staggering, their output of echoes.

I can't help it, I ask them *Why?*
My tall silences. Why they say everything
by being here. By not answering.

It's no use trying not to die in this dream
Streetlights the gold chargers
on my kitchen table   My family surrounds me like statues
in East City Park Their eyes   pockmarks on the sidewalk
filled with rainlight & the sleepcrawl of branches

A man smokes in his doorway downwind
on Blaine   arm swinging like a singlechain thurible
Everything the size of a cathedral   His eyes
bedsprings lonely bodies fall onto in dark basements
Face translucent raw as newborn rabbits
I never see him again

I know myself by the things that scare me
Veins humming in my hands are raised
dark roads   I have been holding tight
onto everything

The night is numbered
in a forest of sharps & flats
In a register where I'm only wet mirrors   It's not important
to know this   Inside me
a silo fills with rain   I sing into it

CHINESE ZODIAC

It must be the work of early-career astronomers
To catalog Neruda's night sky full of roses.
I sway in the street when looking at the moontops of pine.
I am an ox pissing against flowers in a park and quiet
Is light years arriving in a darkwink of leaves.
Rhododendrons, their purpled eyes searching my face.

It is June; I am a dragon
In a twelve-year cycle. According to the placemat in my pocket,
You are eccentric and your life complex. Really,
I am selfish like the rooster, candid like tigers.
I need to avoid the dog.

On nights when the moon fills its ballrooms,
It startles streetlights in the folds of women's dresses.
Memory won't stop happening to me.
I stand at the sink and cry spent horses.
I have held hands in the dark with a rabbit.
Tell me what to do—*Marry a rat late in life.*
There is no animal for the year we meet.

46.7324° N, 117.0002° W

I've become an issue of tense
I am   we were   you are
the missing part   the missed   the two
extra buttons sewn inside my shirt   I press them
now between my ribs

& snow falls on lights of the silos
lengthens wintergrass in my hair
My breath leaves like trainsmoke   dissipates
as lights come on in high windows of the jail

I say *happiness* out loud   that it would be enough
of a prescription   Branches & fire escapes darken
Night slides down the throat of a steeple
I've lost the center   There is no center
Only administrations of houselights & a qualification of bells

Nothing rhymes with *orange* in English except a memory—
a woman with cat eyes buried in moonlight
on a rooftop in Manhattan when she reached   for my hand

Carry me to that woman's ear   to the dimple
of her lower back   that smelled of lilacs & Maldon salt
For now I call November to the sky   all its constellations—
those just being born those just now dying
Really   anything

MYTHOS

Mother, I am wrong—
we are not from stone, but my memories
make hard things of beauty.
          There is a small bird that lives inside me
telling everything backwards to my birth.
There, there, he says and scares
from a wooden table where a chair's been pushed away.
He moves between my ribs, holds them like branches
with a voice that calms horses, like the dark boards of dreams.
In a field outside the town of my youth he waits
like young widows for sleep.
          The name he calls my blood is yours.
He leaves his work in the corners of my eyes,
in drawings on the walls of my mouth
where a man stands in a field, an ornament to moonlight.
Sometimes he lies down, others
he takes a knee, a bath, a life.

FOREST EXERCISES

I am the son of the bird fire that has no eyes but sings to itself after
waiting alone and silent in the alien wood.

—W.S. Merwin

I. My Wild Family

Come down when you hear the chainsaw,
he says as I leave the house.
Our time together, best with work.
Morning through the slatted boards, cuticles of light.
I remember him pleasant, before anger sharpened
as teeth from patterns of wear. His blood's rough edges
run in my wrists. Mice gnawing kindling in the shed—
their god, a hole in the wall to Michigan.

I leave a stream of wet sunlight on the ferns and my stare in the woods.
Music through the walls, classical and muddled.
A doe ten feet away looks up, chews. Doesn't move.
Its eyes shine green as a level's liquid.
A fawn uneven on the path.

His machine grabs in the distance, and my wild family scares.
Father, we bite at trunks and our tongues.
We are slow as trees to forgive.
I am your prince of silence
walking toward the noise in your hands.

II. My Leaving and His

I've learned to listen
for the doorslam, the engine's turn.
In the woods, leaves are still
and thin green faces. I lean
at the jamb of the shed,
my body ages uncontrollably.
Early June, dawn and the sounds begin. The world
unfolding its maptight sleep.
The compass points inward
to the knives of stars, to cardinals of forgetting.
Say *A son's no thing but a map to likeness*. Or don't.
Have I become the way you look to me?
A bird calling to another of its kind—
the answer begins to rain.
It is raining in the darker parts of my body.

III. Dark Cargo

This is the one where I disappear
into syllables of my name, curse handfuls of sparrows
in the poplar, make my body the long thin tongue
of a fly-line licking Michigan dust from leaves.
        I listen to your body speak—

1,000 coughs of convalescents
pushing out a death-air. The black of wet trunks
like men in long coats, their hands leathered in the rain and quick.
I am going somewhere three sentences from safety.
        Who will carry me back?

Rain from April's dark strata
shivers on the leaves as we walk the gravel drive.
There is no dream between us, only my eyes,
two wetted envelopes battening the dusk.
        The license your silence gives me to love you.

My arms, the handles of a wheelbarrow you fill
with hard earth. How we move ourselves,
how we clear the beach, pulling everything green.
Take my hands that you might understand me.
        That I might open to darkness.

IV. Leveling

August. Frankfort. Leveling the birches.
Ribbons on trunks marked for cutting.
You aren't worried about their chances.
High up, thin trees struggle for light—
They've grown toward stronger ones.
I convince you to save a paper birch
(I'd climbed it as a child).
                                        What things!
This forest is not our way to talking.
Above the road you kneel unseen, shout my help for tools
and the wheelbarrow, which I empty at your knees.
You work in the noises at dusk like a factory
shutting down, one light at a time.

I've grown towards you and away from myself.
My shoes fill with sky.
I will not make a lifetime of decisions easy on you,
though I'd take your hand on my back for words.

All this wagering me awake in the world
has only hurt the world. I love
        differently now—
the names I call myself
when you no longer care to be the one I answer to.

PHARAOH

You are asleep,
arms crossed upon your chest.
I whisper to you
blue in TV-light,

collect your breath
in jars, shelve them
inside me.

Nothing waits
except the filth under your nails.

Tomorrow, a doctor
will search your body
for wrong languages dying
to preserve themselves
like kings.

Here I am being something better than rain
Sitting with a cigarette at the back of everything   Apparitionthin
clouds stain my teeth   Gray a vulture coming for me
Mama I've shown it too much
Headlights blur the shine of does' eyes
their shadows cancel branches

There my voice brings nothing back
from Beulah   but the purples of January
I am sick of nature   human or otherwise
Where is a kindness I can mimic

Take my memory scraped raw by lake rock
& latitude Take my nerves   knife gouges in the linoleum

When I sat on the dock this morning asking
for compassion I pretended   the waves were breaths
repeating *Yes*   I saw the heart for what it is
a noisemaker

Of all the things I'm not   I am certain
of echoes   those meridians reaching from forgiveness & love
& that somewhere in the distance they meet

LIKENESS

Talking feels canceled when I stand alone
in the forest. Mother, your thinness is a letter
to my worry. I watch you work in the garden.
I confuse solitude with loneliness.
My hair is also gray kisses at sundown.
A doe strafes the ridgeline until lost
in the thicket, only snapping brush.

God undressed in an arbor of madness;
I am his mannequin's shadow.
My eyes empty the last clip of daylight
into the forest, and quietly
the rain on leaves leaves leaves clean.

You have tried to make me yours;
I think of the bones you broke to bring me here.
I promise. I am trying to love the world.
It is not impossible. Place
your flowers on the sill inside me.

44.6336° N, 86.2345° W

Spirits passing through hair & the linen
shirts of young men smoking in the park
They dream the undergarments   of crabgrass & the despair of leaves
Dewclaws & the milked undersides of cottonwoods
are also dreamt They sweep   cobwebs hanging in pint glasses

speak for pollen & the dead at Pt. Betsie   Decommissioned moonlight
in the Fresnel lens says the heart
when the mouth is cold

I listen by watching   the breakwater's chains
lakers laden with ore   the raspberry's wet curfew
against the calamine of a stripped birch
Behind everything waves   concrete gray & unplaced on faces

I know you're there
Say my life is still   here & reckless
I'll open the canned moonrise with my teeth

SPIRITS, ANIMALS, EASTERN TIME

Their noses like bites from dark plums
root the walled garden for grasses. I
imagine they have no opinions, make
no ritual of sound, their moving so.
Morning unlocked by the jaw of a buck,
winter sleeping in its lightless mouth
for months. I want the relics of their old
gods, to place them on velvet tongues
and wait for the lake to shatter into a
single digit. The trouble with pressure
is where to put it. I've become a voice
packed in salt. Pink increments scatter
like drops of blood in a glass of water.
January scares into the wood of the
deck, and the does leave shadows in the
vacancies they bedded. I don't know
what it is, but I want their myth to enter
me like water where a fish has surfaced.
I move in a cold that is pine and power
outage out-rippling. A spirit parses the
quiet crowns of rutted drives, stalks
the drifts, and shifts its language to the
yard.

41.9740° N, 87.6782° W

When I wake your voice   falls through me
                Years I drew from it on Ravenswood
on Winchester   Your breath no longer written on my chest
        I get closer to the earth on my knees to hear

Tap the window for the sound my body makes
    on its reflection   The sky is forced to listen
        I walk further each day toward the strange
                austerity my heart makes of reason

You are a light I keep   pressed against me The notes
            of dead keys abandoned in my body

    I take the walls apart a brick at a time
        Stack sections of sky behind my eyes
When I close them your language   is a trespassing

That day we took a boat down the river   Did it empty
        into the lake   Did the Manitous lay before us
like tired cubs in the sun   Did we stay through the small hours

            My memories have found ways to travel
in darkness I can hear them now   I move between rooms
                called forgetting my dreams

                I don't know where the day ends
    but that it does when I try   to sleep When I imagine you are
                    & so pretend   to feel close

DISTANT COUNTRY

Memory's as fair as it has to be.
You are the handle of a door opening
to a ballroom lit with fireflies. I live in there
like moths caught in a stack of glasses,
a dream slipped into the west. In the dark
I say *No* to whatever love
                                    I've promised strangers.

I meet madness every morning clean.
Bearded, it waits for me at night.
How many lives I'll undo making you a distant country.
The hills could burn and with them the farmers and the farms.
When I say your name, I say the whole alphabet of my remembering.
God has three letters too, but cannot spell
                                    a moment of my happiness.

Memories are less imaginary—
placing them on Winchester at that window with your face,
waving them in wind that climbs my arm among the trees—
they are inches light and numbered as waves. Smiles are lakes
of bright blue upwards. My sleep, thin as abacus wire—
a dream of the body
                        that inhabits the body.

Each day a map of smoke, and I place you in it.
Where you are even has a name: *Oregon*.
The word sounds like forever
ago in my mouth.
                        I call it the end of the world.

44.6336° N, 86.2345° W

The moon through the pines says shadow
Means my eyes are Gaelic   for dark walls A woman is
combing her hair behind the curtains
in a small house   Her life
warm & yellow   My memory
drinks her sugarsense of hummingbirds

I am the language of nocturnals
Four decades old & whatever
reflection the wind ruins   To the dark
I say my chest upon anything a sunken ship
My weight a boatful of irises   on Inishmore

I can see it I am the shadow   a dog chases I am the dog
Like the ripple of dark water
in a horse's eye I cannot sleep through the night
the month the century

The wind dies too Cam
leaves stillness in the cathedral of Michigan
I think I am   become a watercolor
windows of my insides painted rain   Thirty years ago

I wrote my name in sand not far from here   erased it with my foot
You are three dreams away   When I understood my mind
I lived here
Beautiful & with such little resistance

Acknowledgements

Robert Wrigley, Alexandra Teague, Michael McGriff, and Brian Blanchfield: for everything, thank you.

I am grateful to the editors of the following journals in which some of these poems first appeared, often in earlier versions: *The American Poetry Review, Beloit Poetry Journal, CutBank, Grist, The Harvard Advocate, La Presa, The Meadow, Raleigh Review, Sonora Review, Terrain, Third Coast,* and *Willow Springs.*

Taylor Waring, Caitlin Feldman, Christopher Howell, Polly Buckingham, and the entire Willow Springs Books staff: thank you for your generosity and attention to these poems.

Love and gratitude to my University of Idaho MFA family.

Special thanks to Joe Wilkins, Elizabeth Renker, Katie Darby Mullins, Scott Bugher, Dave DeCastris, Daniel Johnson, Noah Falck, and Michael Landreth.

My Chicago family: thank you.

Maggie Queeney, Bat, and Skel: all my love.

To my family.

Acme Poem Company

Willow Springs Books is a small literary press housed in Eastern Washington University's MFA program in Spokane, Washington. Its annual chapbook series selects and publishes contemporary surrealist poetry under the auspices of the Acme Poem Company.

Willow Springs Books staff who contributed to this chapbook are Mirium Arteaga, Mackenzie Badger, Michelle Brumley, Michael Dundrea, Caitlin Feldman, Corinne Jaeger, and Taylor Waring.

Previous Collections

Black Postcards, Michael McGriff
The 9-Day Queen Gets Lost on Her Way to the Execution, Karyna McGlynn
Startle Pattern, Larissa Szporluk
Drunk on Salt, James Nolan
You Won't Need That, Robert Gregory
Gnawing on a Thin Man, Ray Amorosi
No Time for Dancing, Adam Hammer
Dark Acre, Canese Jarboe
Time Machine, Laura Kasischke

For a complete list of selections from Willow Springs Books and ordering information, visit willowspringsbooks.org.